What's in your heart?

By

Alex Ndukwe

Forward

We are in a time when most people do not mind their hearts and since they give no attention to the very core of their personalities, bankruptcies of character becomes unavoidable. It must be understood that the qualities of our hearts determine to a large extent, the qualities of our lives. No wonder the bible says in Proverbs 4:23 "Keep thy heart with all diligence for out of it are the issues of life".

The heart is the breeding place for all manners of thoughts which form our words, ours words go to form our actions which when engaged in over a long time, form our habits which form our character and character forms our ultimate destiny. No wonder we are implored to apply diligence in the use of our hearts!

The book 'WHAT'S IN YOUR HEART?' is quite a delicious read and at the same time an expository spiritual material on the state of the heart. it is a book that when read, will first become implosive before it becomes explosive in our hearts. the author has ensured that the lines of thoughts contained herein should challenge every reader to not only mind the heart but also profit from this great factory of humanity.

This book is a material that can help every child of God maximize the use of the heart in our everyday living so that he/she can get the best out of our walk with God. I highly recommend this book for every age group as it addresses the bedrock of our collective existence. God bless you.

Pastor Samuel Olatoye Babalola

Pastor-In-Charge of Redeemed Christian Church of God (RCCG), Nassarawa Province 2.

Table of contents

Dedication

This book is dedicated to Pastor Rotimi Nathaniel, Provincial Pastor, Redeemed Christian Church of God (RCCG), Masters Place Parish, Utako, Federal Capital Territory. An erudite bible scholar, he taught this topic in our morning dew (early morning devotion) and I got the inspiration to carry out further research and deliver this book to the glory of God.

Introduction

What's in your heart? , this book asks a question, our society is affected positively or negatively by our individual hearts and we need to be conscious of this. A child of God should affect his society positively but unfortunately there's decay in all strata of our society and the Christians are doing much to salvage the situation, definitely we have not taken our rightful position. Social commentators might want to argue the authenticity of my assertion by demanding for data and my answer will be; all over the world we have a population of 1.3 billion Catholics, 279 million Pentecostal Christians and 260 million orthodox. These figures were released in 2017.

Our focus is on Christians, it is because of the things in our hearts that makes us remain ineffective; our behaviors are not different from unbelievers despite our salvation experience, we form the bulk of complainants when the polity does not live up to desired expectation, fear of God and virtues of Christianity has been thrown to the dogs and we are not different from the gentiles.

I am not interested in castigating any denomination, but every Christian has a heart and we need to answer the question this book is asking all of us, what is in our individual hearts. we are not left out from nation building, our little contributions is required in this direction and government of the day should not be saddled with this responsibility alone, we are all stakeholders and we must participate.

The bible uses the word heart primarily to refer to the ruling center of the whole person, the spring of all desires, the heart is the 'home of the personal life', and hence a man is designated, according to his heart. Any action that man takes – good or bad is first conceived in the heart, it might take a long process to fine tune the plans before execution. For us to see how important the heart is, the children of Israel to leave Egypt, God had to harden the heart of pharaoh, this made the work easy, Exodus 4:21:

'And the LORD said unto Moses, When thou goest to return into Egypt, see that thou do all those wonders before Pharaoh, which I have put in thine hand: but I will harden his heart, that he shall not let the people go".

The Lord fulfilled his promise to Moses in Exodus 7:13, '**And he hardened Pharaoh's heart, that he hearkened not unto them**; as the LORD had said. This made the work easy, his continual refusal to release the children of Israel led to the use of force so as to ensure the migration never took place & this led to their destruction, while the children of Israel decided to move, this made pharaoh and his army go after them towards the red sea, Exo 14:4-5 , '**And I will harden Pharaoh's heart, that he shall follow after them; and I will be honoured upon Pharaoh, and upon all his host; that the Egyptians may know that I am the LORD.** And they did so.

And it was told the king of Egypt that the people fled: and the heart of Pharaoh and of his servants was turned against the people, and they said, why have we done this, that we have let Israel go from serving us? Pharaoh and his large army went after them until they got to the red sea, Moses stretched his rod on the red sea, the lord cause the sea to go back with a strong east wind, made it a dry land and divided the water into two and the children of Israel passed over the dry land and the Egyptian army followed on the same route, the lord troubled the Egyptians through the pillar of fire and cloud , took off their chariot wheel. The Lord instructed Moses to stretch his rod over the sea, the waters came together and destroyed the Egyptians.

The lesson from this story is that, pharaoh's heart was hardened by God and led him to aggression against the children of Israel. He would have continued to dialogue with Moses for them to stay. Forgiveness is propelled by the heart, most times it ends up on our lips but not from inner most heart, then this forgiveness is not total, and this fellow constitutes bondage of him/herself and this leads to sin against God.

What's in your Heart

A criminal conceives the purported crime in his/her heart before it's committed, various permutations are also analyzed with respect to the risks involved. 'Create in me a clean heart, O God; and renew a right spirit within me. Cast me not away from thy presence; and take not thy holy spirit from me. ' Our hearts has to be pure, Mathew 5:8, says 'Blessed are the pure in heart: for they shall see God.' , psalm 51:10-11 , the psalmist talks about God creating a new heart and renew a right spirit within us' , a pure heart will see God , the holy Spirit would dwell richly in us and this has diverse implications because we can have access to vital information from the throne of grace and this will make a huge difference in our life's.

We need to ensure that our hearts are filled with positive thoughts and ensure that it does not hover around anything negative , but let's be practical , but there are sometimes we have unpleasant experience and negative thoughts flow into our hearts, at this point we must remain positive & focused at all times , no matter what the situation is.   Having absolute control of our emotions is also very vital, the condition of our heart determines this and we need to be conscious of this fact.

Chapter One

Describing the heart

The heart is defined in the dictionary as 'a hollow muscular organ that pumps the blood through the circulatory system by rhythmic contraction and dilation. In vertebrates there may be up to four chambers (as in humans), with two atria and two ventricles.' This implies that it's the most vital organ in the human body, without it there won't be life, in spiritual parlance the heart determines how far we can go with God in terms of success, progress that an individual will make in life and that is the more reason why it's described as the engine room of our destiny.

According to the psalmist in Psalms 86:11 says:

'Teach me your way, O LORD, and I will walk in Your truth. Grant me undividedness of heart so that I may fear your name.'

That means the heart can be divided. In that condition, we get pulled in different directions, we go up and then we go down, we blow hot and cold, we are lukewarm, neither hot or cold. We are subject to too much external influence, times of inner peace interspersed with times of inner conflict. You feel saved today and unsaved tomorrow, ever learning but never coming to the knowledge of the truth. Not able to make enough progress, because of too much encumbrance.

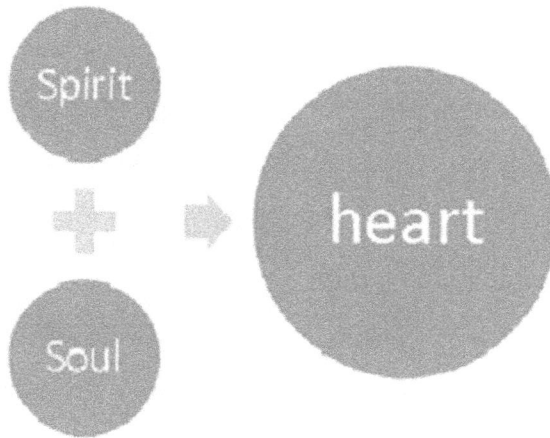

The man with a divided heart may have a sin that beset him on which he or she trips, impeding his spiritual journey. A sinful heart is disconnected from the almighty and this indicates that the heart is not pure; Mathew 5:8 says only the pure in heart will see God, meaning the presence of the Holy Spirit.

According to the diagram above the spirit and the soul makes up the heart. The heart is incomplete without the spirit. Paul called the heart without the spirit darkened (Romans 1:21, Ephesians 4:18).

'For although they knew God, they neither glorified Him as God nor gave thanks to Him, but they became futile in their thinking and darkened in their foolish hearts.' 'They are darkened in their understanding and alienated from the life of God because of the ignorance that is in them due to the hardness of their hearts.'

That means the light of the knowledge of God is not reflected there (2Corinthians 4:6), the presence of God is not manifest there, the name of Jesus is not glorified there, God has no dwelling there because God is light and in him there is no darkness at all (1John 1:5). Does the holy state of the heart make it impossible for one to commit error? Not necessarily. Remember that the heart, and specifically the soul part, has learned some patterns of behavior, there are some behavioral encoding, cultural and social conditioning, emotional programming, and experiential pre-settings. That is why renewal of the mind (a component of the soul) is important Romans 12:2,

'And be not conformed to this world: but be ye transformed by the renewing of your mind, that ye may prove what is that good, and acceptable, and perfect, will of God.'

Let's look at Ephesians 4:22-24,

'That ye put off concerning the former conversation the old man, which is corrupt according to the deceitful lusts; And be renewed in the spirit of your mind; And that ye put on the new man, which after God is created in righteousness and true holiness.'

Renewal of the mind is very essential, we know that cars require maintenance for it to be in top shape and perform better, the inner mind requires service and this is a result of a child of God attending church programme, seminars, conferences, prayer meetings this supports our quest with respect to ensuring that our spirit man is revived, the frequencies of such meetings must be on the rise , since we must tarry in his vineyard. Some school of thought are of the opinion that one could attend church programme and still remain cold in the spirit, yes this is possible, the word of God aids this process, the crux of the matter is that such words should be received by faith, the fellow must be willing to surrender all to Jesus by ensuring the flesh does not override and negate transformation that this process offers.

The new man must be enthroned, the flesh must be dead to sin and nothing more, we must not forget that we have different kind of Christians, i.e. ceremonial, eye-service, real child of God and at this stage we must know where we belong. A real child of God would have focus on God at the point of renewal of mind and the others are neither here or there, they want to be noticed, a typical descendant of the Pharisees and the lord will help us in the name of Jesus.

The reason the focus is on the mind and not the will or the emotion, two other components of the soul is that, while the emotion can be moved and the will can be forced, the mind holds the key to long-lasting change and transformation. We are told to exercise, eat well and manage our stress. These are all important measures to care for our physical heart as we are regularly reminded by members of the medical profession. What does our Creator tell us about caring for our heart? For that, we'll need to look into the Bible, his guidebook for living life? Guarding your heart means to forgive others who may have hurt you.... to let go of any anger, bitterness and resentment toward another that you may have and to release their hurtful behavior or words they may have spoken to you. Make allowance for each other's faults and forgive anyone who offends you, col 3:13 forbearing one another, and forgiving one another, if any man have a quarrel against any:

even as Christ forgave you, so also do ye.' Remember, the Lord forgave you, so you must forgive others, no matter what had transpired, we agree words are like egg dropped on the floor, it might not be retrieved, we must learn to forgive and not put ourselves in bondage. Our minds and heart are intricately connected. What we think about affects our inner spirit and heart. The Bible tells us to think about things that are pure and right and heavenly. When we do this, it creates a healthy environment for the rest of the body. In almost magical ways, these good thoughts sink deep into our being and have an impact on our nervous system and endocrine system. The hormones that are released in our bodies when we think good thoughts are heart-healthy, as opposed to the harmful hormones that are released when we are thinking negative thoughts. Proverbs 17:22 says that a merry heart doeth good like a medicine: but a broken spirit drieth the bones. We must endeavour to be cheerful at all times , it will benefit us, we cannot divulge the human nature that tends to bring about sorrow when an incidence that is not in our favour occurs, as believers we need to guard against this when it occurs.

Chapter two

Scriptural Accounts

The encounter between Cain and Abel in Genesis chapter 4:3-7, the brothers gave their offering unto the Lord. The Almighty had respect for Abel's offering because of the quality while that of Cain'was of poor quality, let's look at verse 6,

'And the Lord said unto Cain, why art thou wroth? And why is Thy countenance fallen?'

Cain obviously was angry, and he developed hatred in his heart over his brother Abel, one would have expected Cain to improve the quality of his offering when the opportunity comes up, Cain killed his younger brother, this action he had taken is unnecessary. This implies that he had always developed a wicked heart before this incidence occurred; he made himself available for the enemy to use him to carry out this abominable act. Samson is another bible character that was destined to be great, unfortunately despite his endowments, he did not fulfill his destiny.

...The prophecy was released to his mother by the angel of the Lord before his birth, For, lo, thou shalt conceive, and bear a son; and no razor shall come on his head: for the child shall be a Nazarite unto God from the womb: and he shall begin to deliver Israel out of the hand of the Philistines... (Judges 13:5)

Samson desired a woman from Timnath, a philistine and from the camp of the enemy, though he shared the idea with his parents, they discouraged him and asked him if there are no women among their brethren .In his heart he had conceived the having a beautiful wife and preferred a philistine, he believed no evil can befall him considering his strength. He defeated the philistine and they discovered he had enormous strength. Judges 16:4, 'And it came to pass afterward, that he loved a woman in the valley of Sorek, whose name was Delilah.' They knew his weakness and they set a trap for him,

Delilah was that trap. It should not surprise us, already in his heart he had always loved beautiful ladies, the Lord of the philistines had a meeting with Delilah and detailed her to find out the secret of his power, this will aid his destruction as he had become a torn in their flesh.

The assignment was carried out and destiny as the deliverer over the philistine was terminated. What he had conceived in his heart right from time, led to his destruction.

Nehemiah, an outstanding bible character, he had a good heart, never gave up, very positive in nature. He had always conceived in his heart to be a game changer for the land of Israel. We must appreciate such attitude in his heart, he believed in this scripture Jerimiah 32:27,

'Behold, I am the LORD, the God of all flesh is   there anything too hard for me?'

He believed that there is nothing that God cannot do, he made frantic efforts to ensure that the walls of Jerusalem that was destroyed is rebuilt.

First and foremost, he met the king and asked for a letter to the Governor for assistance with respect to the task ahead, he encountered difficulties: Nehemiah 2:10 **"When Sanballat the Horonite, and Tobiah the servant, the Ammonite, heard of it, it grieved them   exceedingly that there was come a man to seek the welfare of the children of Israel.'** Despite the challenges faced by Nehemiah, in verse 20, **'Then answered I them, and said unto them, The God of heaven, he will prosper us; therefore, we his servants will arise and build: but ye have no   portion, nor right, nor memorial, in Jerusalem.'**

How can we describe the heart of the servant of God, Faith in God radiates in his heart, there was no resources to embark on this assignment, help could not come from the Governor across the river, he didn't give up, rather he depended on the most authentic source in the universe, the Almighty, he mobilized his people and the wall was rebuilt.

Judas Iscariot, a disciple of Jesus Christ. How do we describe his heart? His heart is full of deceit, greed & covetousness. People with such heart pretend, they are wolf in sheep skin. The account in John 12:3-6 , let's look at verse 3 and we will now analyze his reaction in verse 5.

'Then took Mary a pound of ointment of spikenard, very costly, and anointed the feet of Jesus, and wiped his feet with her hair: and the house was filled with the odour of the ointment.'

Judas complained what a waste and this ointment could have been sold for 300 pence and the money used to take care of the poor. This man is been tactical in his approach, let us look at verse 6,

'This he said, not that he cared for the poor; but because he was a thief, and had the bag, and bear what was put therein'.

The bible called him a thief, though a disciple and one would have expected so much from him with respect to his behavior, this clearly shows that greed in his heart has made him always want to maximize situation of things around him and he's transactional in nature, meaning he always want to make money from every slightest opportunity that comes his way , such people are around us today. Jesus gave him a very good response in verse 7-8,

'Then said Jesus, Let her alone: against the day of my burying hath she kept this. For the poor always ye have with you; but me ye have not always.'

The response was for him to know that the ointment poured on the feet of Jesus was not a waste After all, but Mary was fulfilling her desire, which shows how precious and important the master was to her & blessings attached to the action. Before the crucifixion, Mathew 26:14-15, Judas met with the chief priest and struck a deal with them that if he delivers Jesus what's will he get as gratification? And they promised him 30 pieces of silver. Mathew 26:48-50, Judas betrayed Jesus,

'Now he that betrayed him gave them a sign, saying, whomsoever I shall kiss, that same is he:

hold him fast. And forthwith he came to Jesus, and said, Hail, master; and kissed him. And Jesus said unto him, Friend, wherefore art thou come? Then came they, and laid hands on Jesus, and took him'.

Judas collected gratification from the chief priest, we shouldn't forget that such monies cannot be used for anything meaningful and at the end of the day how did he end up? He was condemned and he repented, returned the 30 pieces of silver, could not bear the pain of his actions and he hung himself. Vanity upon vanity, Matthew 16:26 says:

'For what is a man profited, if he shall gain the whole world, and lose his own soul? or what shall a man give in exchange for his soul?'

A heart of greed leads to destruction, love for money is the root of all evil, and Judas destroyed himself. The Lamb of God, it's a perfect example that we need to emulate as children of God, I agree that all that transpired during his crucifixion was for the scripture to be fulfilled , the predictions were already reeled out by prophet Isaiah , just a pronouncement and host of angels will deliver him from the clutches of the elders & Roman Governor. Let's leave this aspect and focus on our discussion about Jesus.

It is because of Jesus Christ that we enjoy salvation, those that believe in him are called Christians and we ought to be proud of this. Brethren no controversies, before his earthly ministry he was baptized, sanctified and every Christian pass through this process before commissioning as a church worker that will be groomed to become a minister & pastor someday. An embodiment of Love, Joy, Peace, Compassion, Care, longsuffering, gentleness, goodness, faith, Meekness, temperance. these are fruit of the spirit as recorded in Galatians 5:22-23, above all he could be described as pure in heart. Can you imagine what transpired when 5,000 people were fed by Jesus, Andrew, the link man and disciple of Jesus suggested that they send the multitude away, how can they feed them and how many penny worth of bread & fishes would be purchased. Jesus insisted that he will feed them , it's only a heart filled with compassion that can take such decision and he's aware that God the father is all sufficient and a great provider,, a young lad emerged with 5 barley loaves & 2 fishes , he looked up to heaven, and blessed, and brake the loaves, and gave them to his disciples to set before them; and the two fishes divided he among them all and they did all eat, and were filled. They took up twelve baskets full of the fragments, and of the fishes.

Another encounter at the pool of Bethesda , a man that had infirmities for 38 years , as recorded in the book of John 5:5-8 , Jesus asked him will you be made whole , this implies whether he wants to be healed and one would have expected an emphatic yes from this man and he narrated the story of not having someone to carry him to the river when the angels troubled the water , most of us would have left him alone but the master knew that he desired a transformation and he sent a word to him , instructing him to Rise, take up his bed, and walk and he was made whole.

We must appreciate that it takes a heart of love to touch lives positively no matter who is involved; miracle working pastors commercialize their gifts of healing. This can be attributed to greed in their hearts; we must not forget Mathew 10:8d,

'Freely ye have received, freely give at the end of the day every single glory will return to God the father'.

As pastors, various categories of church workers we must be Christ-like , most people assert that it's difficult to have a heart like Jesus , we must thirst for it and work towards it and ensure we attain this qualities of the master. It is achievable if we remain focused.

Chapter 3

Engine Room of your destiny

The heart remains the engine room of your destiny, this statement is very valid in different perspectives, can you believe that your heart has got eyes, let us look at Ephesians 1: 18.

'Having the eyes of your hearts enlightened, that you may know what the hope of his calling is, and what are the riches of the glory of his inheritance in the saints'.

What are your goals in life? Or perhaps what do you what to achieve in the nearest future, one might even say what dreams do you have? These questions are not for the young adults alone but all of us, there is need for us to challenge ourselves. It now depends on how our hearts will perceive these assertions and how enlightened the eyes of our heart is for it to see , visualize the challenges that could arise while on the journey of reaching the set targets , these eyes will help you to identify these opportunities wherever they are.

We don't just eat, sleep & wake-up on daily basis but we must have goals in our hearts that drives us to achieving success. If you do not have a goal, it is not too late, you can create one today. How positive or negative you are when opportunities comes knocking now depends on what is embedded in your heart, it's been positive all the time could be very beneficial, this will help to douse any negative feeling or comments from any quarter, in a nut shell the heart of such a fellow can see the positives of any negative situation and at the end of the day transformation occurs. A positive heart can never me threatened or challenged by anything negative.

What are the hopes of his calling? , these hopes are enormous and these are bound to make our hearts positive , first and foremost every child of God has the privilege to be choosing and ordained , John 15:16a ,

'Ye have not chosen me, but I have chosen you, and ordained you'.

A relationship is invoked by every child of God , it's pertinent to note that we need to ensure that standard set are maintained and sustained so as to guarantee a cordial relationship , when you are chosen he now sees you   As a friend, John 15:15 ,

'Henceforth I call you not servants; for the servant knoweth not what his lord doeth: but I have called you friends; for all things that I have heard of my Father I have made known unto you'

Thus, as Christians, we should be filled with hope because we know that God has called us to salvation. Our faith in Christ did not originate with our feeble will, but with the sovereign, eternal will of God. We know that He will fulfill all His promises to us. We will be with Him forever in heaven, where there will be no suffering or tears or death. We will be perfect in righteousness and in love for God and one another.

The promises are enormous and are embedded in our bibles , God is not man that he should lie, this implies that these promises are sure

, condition of our heart determines if we will access it or not , as Christians we need to thirst for a new heart, psalm 51:10 says 'Create in me a clean heart, O God; and renew a right spirit within me.' , the heart must be clean at all times no matter what the situation is or challenges you are facing , never allow any form of impurities to reside there.

The promises will be accessed via faith & the heart is vital , you can now imagine a heart filled with hatred, what kind of faith will such a fellow exercise, rather   there will be a disconnect spiritually , this individual will continue to revolve in circles without results.   Can we take a typical example, Mr A loses a possession and promise is found in the book of Joel 2:25 ,

'And I will restore to you the years that the locust hath eaten, the cankerworm, and the caterpillar, and the palmerworm, my great army which I sent among you'.

Before we continue let's look at the story in 2Kings 8:4-6.

'And the king talked with Gehazi the servant of the man of God, saying, Tell me, I pray thee, all the great things that Elisha hath done. And it came to pass, as he was telling the king how he had restored a dead body to life, that, behold, the woman, whose son he had restored to life, cried to the king for her house and for her land. And Gehazi said; My lord, O king, this is the woman, and this is her son, whom Elisha restored to life.

And when the king asked the woman, she told him. So the king appointed unto her a certain officer, saying, Restore all that was hers, and all the fruits of the field since the day that she left the land, even until now.'

Apart from these promises, this a classical example of restoration, the Shunammite woman lost her son and Elisha was the vessel God used for the restoration of the son, this woman had previously told the prophet don't tease me, she never believed she could ever have a child , the miracle came to pass , the woman has always had a positive heart and this is the proof in 2Kings 4:26 ,

'Run now, I pray thee, to meet her, and say unto her, Is it well with thee? is it well with thy husband? Is it well with the child?

And she answered, 'It is well.' She answered the prophet that it well with his son despite the fact that this boy was lifeless, if you were in her shoes what will you do? , you might even scream at the man of God, if she didn't believe that miracle can still take place she wouldn't have gone to the man of God for assistance, she would have taken it as her destiny, the heart of this woman was full of positives and her spirit man ready for a supernatural connection. The miracle came to pass. This miracle was a connection to another restoration, her landed properties that were seized, in 2 king 8: 4, the king was asking Gehazi the servant of the prophet for information of the great miracles that Elisha had done and he told the king of a woman that the son was raised from the dead , the woman appeared and Gehazi pointed at her , the King was excited and this brought her in contact with the king and don't forget Proverbs 21:1 says

'The king's heart is in the hand of the LORD, as the rivers of water: he turneth it whithersoever he will'

The Lord used the king to restore all her landed properties, what an awesome God. In Christendom we have not taken our rightful place, rather we continue to deceive ourselves, in chapter 2 , it's stated that the soul & spirit makes up the heart. Most hearts are filthy & how can miracle take place when there is a disconnection.

the schematic diagram Figure A and Figure B will aid our discussion , from these diagrams every one claims to exhibits faith and this is the currency that is available to every child of God to access the supernatural , unfortunately the state of the heart determines if miracle will happen or not. A good Filthy Heart Faith Miserable

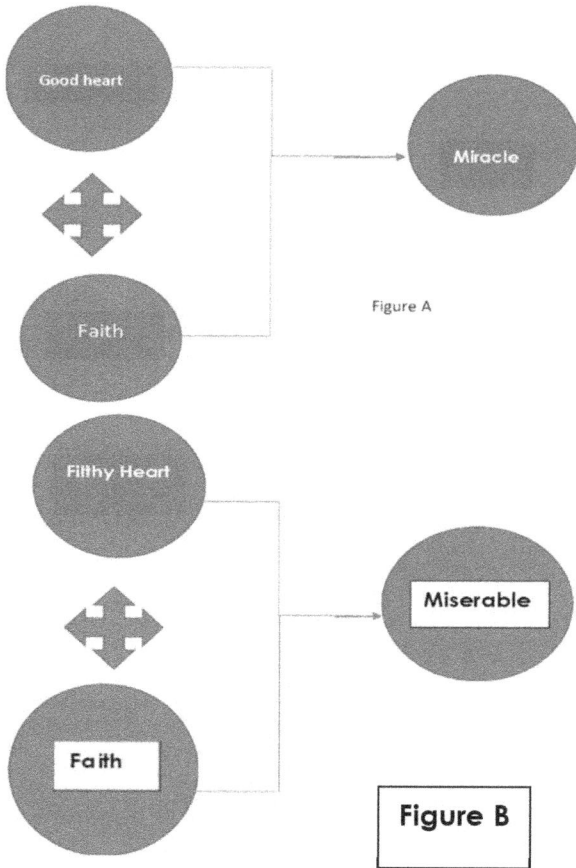

Figure A

Figure B

Heart is one with positives spiced with faith, even if it's like a mustard seed would lead to miracle.

In Nigeria due to depression, there is high rate of suicide, the victims are described by figure B, I quite agree they could exhibit faith but the heart is filled with negatives, the heart can only see the physical challenges and cannot view the likely transformation that could occur spiritually. Can we remember the business tycoon that attempted jumping into the Lagoon, she was arrested by rapid response squad and they asked her why are you attempting suicide? she was in debt to her suppliers in Switzerland and her family had forsaken her, and she met her pastor, he simply prayed for her and told her all will be well, according to her it's better she leaves the scene. The faith is just on her lips and not in her heart, she cannot see beyond the debts she's owing and her heart is filled with things like what a disgrace for me, how do I face this embarrassment, How will I raise such a huge amount of money etc , this spells catastrophe , what has happened to the promises of God , such hearts will not remember anything called promises when there is a challenge.

Jesus speaks about the seed of the gospel and its life-changing ability falling on the fertile ground of a "noble and good heart" with the resulting fruit and life change. Well, we want to ask, what kind of heart is that heart of flesh that Ezekiel promised that God would be giving us? What kind of heart is "the pure of heart" that Jesus talks about in the beatitudes in Matthew 5's Sermon on the Mount? Let's look so that we can test our own. As Christians we must examine ourselves and we need to ask this simple question, 'How is your heart? Nancy Beach once delivered a seminar at the Willow Creek church in Chicago for pastors, she stated that there are five key indicators that will help us see the health of our heart and soul, our spiritual condition. They are as follows:

1. Emotions

2. Moments

3. Fun

4. People

5. Whispers.

Let's look at the details of the breakdown stated above for clarity purpose, below are the excerpts from the seminar:

1. Emotions

A healthy heart experiences emotions. A healthy person cries at times and laughs at times. A healthy heart is touched by joy, pain, anger, gratitude and love. So, having said that, I ask you to ask yourselves, "Have I cried over anything lately?" or "Have I really laughed?" A healthy heart is touched by the pain of others as well as personal pain. A healthy heart experiences emotional change when it's happening. Someone suggested that Elijah's heart, when he was running from Jezebel, was not at all healthy anymore. After all, he wished to die and then fell asleep. That's more a state of numbness, incapable of feeling anymore. Truly a heart that has some major blockage, waiting for a total seizure. So, think about it. How would you rate your capacity to feel deep emotion? Rating it from a high (5) to a medium (3) or a low (1)? Let's move on with our heart check. I'm eager to have us look at the other four checks too.

2. Moments

Author Frederick Buechner advises us: "Listen to your life...all moments is key moments and life itself is grace." Oh, how often we fail to seize the moments that God provides. We fail to seize the day as given. We wait instead for what doesn't come. We're not in the present and instead we dwell on the past or anticipate the future, and the whole time, we're missing out on the present. When our hearts are working right, when we do what we are intended to do, we can look each other in the eye and relish each moment. Then we're not in such a destructive hurry to move on that we miss the present moment. We learn to listen to our children, to our friends, to our partners, as well as our parents. We savor the present. We see the shine in our children's eyes when they tell us something exciting, show us something new, and share a happening. We do so without trying to be somewhere else.

A healthy heart savors the present and doesn't skim through it. It's mindful of what is happening and relishing it for what it is. With this in mind, ask your children or others close to you, "Are you all there for them?" Ask yourself, how would you rate your moment mindfulness? From a 5 to a 1? From the high to the low? Where are you? Our next one is a challenger too. Let's learn together.

3. Fun

Life can be so overwhelming! So much can be demanding your time. Needs may pile up. We get worn out and all too serious with life. Again, a healthy heart has the capacity as well as the need to laugh, to relax, and to enjoy life's events. Jesus came to give life and give it to the full. John 10:10 tells us that rather clearly, and we used to say He came to give it "abundantly" what now we call "to the full." Either way you translate it, it means to live life as God intended us to do so. When we can no longer play, no longer laugh, or simply let go, then we're asking for a heart failure, a collapse. You might call it burn-out. You can call it life fatigue. Whatever you call it, it's devastatingly destructive. Do you set some time aside for sports, quiet reading, or something that's a change from your routine? Think about it, and rate yourself again with the fun factor. High, medium, or low. What are you risking? The next factor is one that ties closely to church fellowship too. Let's move on.

4. People

How are you seeing people? When Jesus saw crowds, he would have compassion on them. He was grieved to tears with the death of his friend Lazarus as he looked at death's pain and destruction. How do you look at people? Do you find people and their problems overwhelming? Do you resent phone calls asking for help? Are you dodging all requests for help?

A healthy heart is empathetic. It listens to the hurts of others. It's willing to take some time to walk a mile with the one hurting, listening and learning that life can be so overwhelming, oh so difficult for others too. Now that does not mean no boundaries in your life. That would be destructive too. But, after all, when all is said and all is done, by what standard will you be judged? "The greatest of these is love!" is still God's standard. Have you loved people? Have you been moved by someone else's lustiness? Measure yourself once again. How loving have you been lately? What you did last year doesn't count! Where do you fit? High, medium or low? On that scale of 5-1, where do you really fi?. Where would your friend put you? The final factor is a more subtle one. Let's look at it now.

5. Whispers

Recall again that Elijah heard God in "the still, small voice!" Does God have to get a megaphone to get your attention? God speaks in a variety of ways, but are we listening? Am I? He is always with us. We claim that promise that Jesus made as He gave the great commission. Then, hear Him speak to you, everywhere and always. God is speaking to us. Sometimes He does so at the most awkward times. Sometimes He does so in what we would think of as most unusual ways.

This examination requires that we be truthful to ourselves, in some cases someone close to you can equally help you in this assessment and this will help us improve the state of our heart , criticism can be beneficial for some of us that are willing and desires improvements. There is good news for some of us that will fall below expectation, there is no condemnation but the heart can be recreated and we can work towards an improvement and we will be positioned for greatness , we need to be ourselves and not that we are not counterfeit but original in the sight of our creator. Seek out what God wants you to do. There'll be joy in your life when you do so. You are God's special work, unique, a once-in-an-eternity person.   Destinies can be achieved, thwarted or destroyed; these depend on the kind of heart that we possess as an individual.

A successful businessman must have built strong and robust relationship with associates in his line of business, this can be narrowed down to suppliers, customers, financial institutions etc, the promoter must have a fertile heart that will ensure that the word of God penetrates and bear fruits that can be seen by others and most importantly such hearts will be willing to learn and understudy new strategies that is bound to improve the fortunes of the enterprise. Spiritually the holy spirit dwells in pure hearts, classified information are available and this makes the venture outstanding, working blindly or with human knowledge can be disastrous and counterproductive, the ideal situation with the help of the holy spirit is that the venture should outlive the founder, many generations will be part of it , can we visualize when corporations like Cocoa cola, Cadbury , Lever brothers , Nestle were founded , many generations have been part of it.

Let's discuss further, what makes one a successful pastor? , we are fully aware of the indices that is usually used for appraisal such as attendance, impartation , miracles performed, quality   programmes organized and other perceptions by the congregations, you might hear words like he doesn't know how to preach, he's not polished , his dressing is very poor etc.

What's in your Heart

A pastor that has a pure heart like our Lord Jesus Christ filled with the fruits of the spirits as mentioned in the book of Galatians 5:22-23 , the holy spirits dwells richly with this pastor and the assignments at hand becomes very easy to accomplish and every decision that will be taken wouldn't be according to flesh , that ministry will blossom and the attendance will increase astronomically and you will hear comments like God is here , the focus must be on the people , they must be disciple, nurtured , trained and make them useful to God. But today the focus has shifted to building physical structures and we must learn from the collapse of Christianity in the advanced countries, these structures have been converted to shopping malls, Night clubs , warehouses etc. , they are paying a price for not building their congregation , the youths will someday become elders , a loss of focus led to this. I have come to realize that building cathedrals, church development, provision of infrastructures had been my primary focus in ministry but this not progress rather building, teaching, and impacting lives positively should be our main focus. The ministers/workers can destroy the leader and most importantly as discussed, the pastor must have a pure heart, and this cannot be compromised. Interestingly we have different kind of pastors, this is not our primary focus of this book, that's for another day.

How many Christian homes can be described as successful, though I agree that many factors are usually considered, but let us not forget that the Man and wife are principal characters that determines whether a home will be successful or not, behavioral patterns are very important and this depends on the hearts involved, most times there is no balance , it might turn out to be one-sided and the couples continue to struggle and endure relationship that lasts for several years.

The characters having quality hearts robs on the children and you will now see a good Christian home where there is love, happiness, fear of God and this becomes an example to other homes. The secret is a pure heart and nothing more. It takes an open heart to open up your earth and if your heart is closed, your earth will be closed. What the engine is in a car is what the heart is to a destiny. Destiny will crash if the heart is broken. The race of life will slow down and be scuttled if the engine is not sound, keep your heart to secure your destiny, Prov.4:23,

'Keep thy heart with all diligence; for out of it are the issues of life.'

Conclusions

Can we imagine the grounds we can cover as Christians if our hearts are pure but unfortunately we are saddled with spiritual heart disease that has rendered us ineffective and made us not to access our blessings that are accrued to most of us, we are children of God without outstanding testimonies and we must take our rightful position in the society.

The Bible indicates a great deal about the condition of the average person's heart. In Proverbs 6:18, the Bible speaks of a "heart that deviseth wicked imaginations." In other words, the Bible says that your heart is full of evil imaginations. And the Bible says, in Jeremiah 17:9, that "the heart is deceitful above all things, and desperately wicked: who can know it?" Your heart is deceitful. You can't trust it, if you're outside of Jesus Christ.

Jesus said, in Matthew 15:8, that our hearts are far from God: "This people draweth nigh unto me with their mouth, and honoureth me with their lips, but their heart is far from me." Think of it now. There are many of you here today who go to church. You sing on Sunday morning. You go through the ritual of the liturgy of your church. With your mouth, you honor God. But your heart is far from Him. Your heart—your real self—is taken up with the things of this world.

We need to invest quality time reading the bible & meditating in the word of God, worshiping God, tarry in the place of Prayer, unfortunately our hearts are far from these spiritual exercises rather we can spend more time watching movies, reading novels , etc., we need to turn a new leaf , this will help us to build our spiritual muscle and revitalize our hearts. Now, what is God's attitude toward our hearts? The Bible says He knows the heart: "Shall not God search this out? For he knoweth the secrets of the heart" (Psalm 44:21). He knows all your secrets. You don't hide anything from God. He knows everything that goes on there. Brethren we need to stop pretending and deceiving ourselves, the Lord knows the intent of our hearts , bible indicates that we need to be a living sacrifice, roman 12:1 ,

'I beseech you therefore, brethren, by the mercies of God, that ye present your bodies a living sacrifice, holy, acceptable unto God, which is your reasonable service.'

, this standard cannot be compromised, a good heart cannot reside in a filthy body and we should take note of this. We need to strife for a good heart , ensure it's always revitalized at all times , this guarantees a great future for us , our lives will never remain the same and when people see you, the glory of God will be evident in your life and you become a worthy examples that men/women will emulate. For those of us with dirty hearts, does not lose hope because God can help you and transformation can occur, remain blessed in the name of Jesus.

www.ingramcontent.com/pod-product-compliance
Lightning Source LLC
Chambersburg PA
CBHW020956030426
42339CB00005B/125